'Oui' or 'Non'?

101 WAYS TO KNOW IF YOUR CAT IS FRENCH

How To Talk to Your Cat About Their Secret Life and Learn The Art of Being French, A Funny Cat Book and The Perfect Gift for Cat Lovers and Those Who Love France

Seamus Mullarkey

DON'T MISS THIS SPECIAL BONUS

GET YOUR FREE BOOK TODAY...

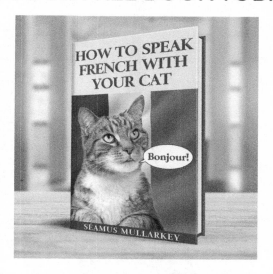

IT'S SO SIMPLE – AND TOTALLY FREE!
– SCAN THE CODE OR CLICK THE LINK....

subscribepage.io/7565d5

INTRODUCTION

Do you have a lingering suspicion that your cat is hiding something from you? Do you think that behind their piercing gaze and twitching whiskers, some long-held truth is yet to be revealed? The answer could be that your cat is actually French. Is it possible that you really have a 'chat' who would be more at home in a French château or a Parisian pied- à-terre? *Meow oui!* Every cat owner knows that their pet has its own particular quirks, but what if their purr-sonality was even more Purr-risian than you could have ever dreamed? If your little bundle of fur is more interested in champagne than catnip then you could be the proud owner of one very French cat.

It isn't always easy to tell at first if your feline is French. Cats are aloof by nature, but they may not be ignoring you... they just might not understand English very well! Communication barriers are common between pets and their humans, but in your kitties' case, they may be even more of an issue than you think. Fortunately for you, if you've been meaning to purchase a French phrasebook, your intrepid kitty may be the best study buddy around. From enjoying French films to discussing Impressionistic art from all of the great French painters, your cat may already be in-the-know.

As much of a fantasy as it seems, your access to a true French lifestyle could be closer to home than you ever imagined. Cats tend to be natural trendsetters, so it isn't surprising just how ahead of you they may be when it comes to living life the French way. After all, doesn't the idea of a gorgeous cat lounging at a cute little cafe without a care in the world sound like both a French and a feline thing to do? The French have a natural sophistication that others can't help but be drawn to. The idea of savoring life and enjoying fine food, art, and sophistication as the French do is like a sparkling dream to many of us.

However, don't sign up for French lessons with your cat just yet! You need to be sure, which is why I've created this highly scientific book that has been rigorously tested under laboratory conditions. You see, there are 101 ways for you to know for sure if you should change Fluffy's name to 'Amelie' or 'Jacques.' Read on, and you may discover that your cat's penchant for the finer French things may be more than fur deep. So, let's travel through the glamour of France from the comfort of your home and in the company of your dear, sophisticated 'chat.'

1

It prefers Perrier.

2

Instead of laying like a loaf of
bread, it croissants.

3

When you promise it a new cat
tower, it expects this one.

4

It thinks its portrait should be in Louvre, next to the Mona Lisa.

5

*If it weren't a carnivore, this would
be its carb of choice.*

6

Like Marie-Antoinette, it declares, "let them eat cake!"

7

It knows you eat with the eyes as well as the stomach...

8

. . .and, it insists on formal table settings.

9

It plays with <u>this</u> football...

10

. . .and not this one.

11

It thinks of five weeks' vacation as standard.

12

Whenever it breaks something,
it gives you a look that says,
"Moi?"

13

It frequents little neighborhood shops – and <u>never</u> big-box stores!

14

It lives for l'amour.

15

It loves a promenade "en bicyclette," but...

16

*...it secretly dreams of competing
in The Tour de France.*

17

It wants to buy books from the stalls in the streets of Paris and <u>not</u> online.

18

It eats rich food but somehow stays slim.

19

It knows how to lounge seductively.

20

It watches French shows on Netflix — without subtitles.

21

Fresh treats from the patisserie make it smile.

22

It wishes you had a bidet, for, well, you know where...

23

It likes long lunches.

24

It thinks nothing of spending hours in a cafe.

25

It shouts "Vive la Revolution!" on Bastille Day.

26

It counts in French, so it's 'un, deux, trois.'.

27

It can analyze the notes in your
new perfume from 50 meters away.

28

It tends to be rather bureaucratic.

29

It does everything with a certain finesse.

30

Its extensive beauty regime keeps it young.

31

It spends hours on park benches contemplating "la vie moderne."

32

It loves to wander along cobblestone streets.

33

It knows how to accessorize.

34

You don't mind if it wakes you early because of its charming "bonjour."

35

It has a certain "je ne sais quoi".

36

*It makes anything it
wears look chic.*

37

It knows how to tie a scarf with flair.

38

It pouts like Brigitte Bardot.

39

It knows how to wear haute couture.

40

It prefers a scooter to an SUV.

41

It loves spending time with poodles — French or otherwise...

42

It goes topless when it sunbathes.

43

It spends August in St Tropez.

44

It perks up if anybody says "aperitif."

45

It looks as if it'd enjoy a hearty Burgundy...

46

It sways in time to accordion music.

47

It dreams of playing 'l'accordéon' itself one day...

48

It's comfortable hob-nobbing at elegant soirées.

49

It spends hours in the bathroom arranging its coiffure.

50

It wants to ride in one of those little French cars.

51

It's all about "liberté, égalité, fraternité", but not so much for dogs...

52

It's such an intellectual, even about the most ordinary things...

53

It can't believe you're so obvious and naive.

54

It thinks of fresh flowers as a necessity.

55

*It sometimes gets so terribly
bored. . .and overcome with 'ennui.'*

56

It likes the loud, screechy jazz music played in French nightclubs.

57

*It dreams of creating a perfume
that smells of boeuf bourguignon.*

58

*It looks as if it's trying to grow
one of those little French mustaches.*

59

It critiques all your outfits.

60

And then suggests alternatives...

61

It knows if it's real champagne.

62

It prances around the house like it's at the Paris Fashion Week.

63

It yearns for a lost love.

64

It knows it's all about the presentation.

65

It can identify 50 different French cheeses with just one taste.

66

It inspects everything you eat or drink as if it's awarding Michelin stars.

67

*It thinks all those
French mimes are funny.*

68

It prefers an herbal 'tisane' to teabags from the supermarket.

69

When it's time to salute the flag, it thinks of this one.

70

It's 'très sportif.'

71

It often seems like it's watching passers-by stroll along Parisian boulevards.

72

It wants you to read it French poetry for hours on end.

73

If it doesn't get what it wants, "c'est tragique!"

74

It dreams of shopping in those glamourous Paris boutiques.

75

It embraces the beauty of the nude form.

76

When you mispronounce a French word, it gives you this look.

77

It wants you both to dress like Marie Antoinette.

78

It adores 'le ballet.'

79

It doesn't think much of microwave meals—"quelle horreur!"

80

It treasures "la tendresse."

81

It thinks you're rude if you don't greet it with "Bonjour Monsieur!" or "Bonjour Madame!"

82

It hates when you use clichés.

83

It greets its friends with a kiss on the cheek.

84

It's so <u>avant-garde</u>.

85

It shows its friends how to apply rouge for "that French look."

86

It can't believe the size of American portions.

87

In its photographs, it looks like the star of an old French film.

88

It's considering busking for small change and living "la vie de bohème."

89

You suspect it spent one of its previous lives dancing at the <u>Moulin Rouge.</u>

90

It prefers the stairs to the elevator.

91

It despises flip-flops anywhere but on the beach.

92

It gives you this look when you say
'fries' instead of 'frites.'

93

It wants to travel to Paris and gaze at the majestic waters of the Seine.

94

It insists on regular spa days.

95

It prefers lavender fields over catnip.

96

Its fur is as smooth as French caramel cake.

97

Although it looks like a plain ole alley cat, it dreams of a château in the Loire Valley.

98

When you say "Cat in The Hat," it runs to put on a beret.

99

It wants to know precisely how its food is prepared.

100

It hunts, but for escargots.

101

It dreams of "La vie en rose."

102

*And it never says goodbye…
just 'au revoir!'*

...à bientôt! See you soon!

CONCLUSION

After a trip to the market, a bicycle ride around town, and lazy afternoons at the beach, this feline tour of France has come to an end. Just how French did your kitty turn out to be? Do they tend to sleep in the shape of a *croissant* more than the typical loaf of bread? Or, do they cuddle with you as a sign of their unending *amour*? Perhaps your four-legged companion has surprised you with just how cultured and chic they are! In that case, you could certainly look forward to practicing living the *French way* together.

And never fear if any of the traits came as a shock to both of you– there are always new and exciting lessons to be learned, whether it be from the French or your cat. They may be onto something with *gourmet escargot*... for your palate or your cat's.

So now what do you do? No need to dress your cat in a beret or feed them baguettes! Simply respect your cat for their fabulous French feline purr-sonality! Perhaps you could even learn French from your cat. Who knows? Behind each purr, meow and trill is a love language full of *je ne sais quoi*. Speak to your kitty in French and see just how responsive your furry little friend can be! We hope that these insights have helped you to better understand your French-speaking kitty friend no matter what part of the globe they call home.

DON'T MISS THIS SPECIAL BONUS

GET YOUR FREE BOOK TODAY...

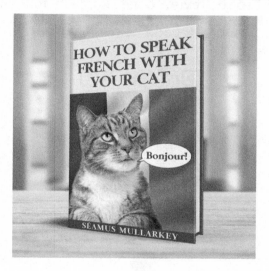

IT'S SO SIMPLE – AND TOTALLY FREE!
– SCAN THE CODE OR CLICK THE LINK....

subscribepage.io/7565d5

Please leave a review...

If this book brought you a few moments of pleasure, I'd be so grateful if you took just a few moments to leave a review on the book's Amazon page.

You can get to the review page simply by following the link

or QR code below. Thanks!

Purrr-leeze leave a review!

About the Author

A cat fanatic and book lover, I write fascinating books about our beloved kitties and how they've shaped our world.

— If you love cats, you'll love my books —

So, why not join my "Cats of the World" fan club? You can read all my new books FOR FREE?

AND... You'll get a free bonus book, "How to Speak French With Your Cat"...

SIMPLY SCAN THE CODE OR CLICK THE LINK TO JOIN!
There's no cost to you

subscribepage.io/7565d5

More from Seamus Mullarkey

Would you like to read more of my books???
Just click or scan below...

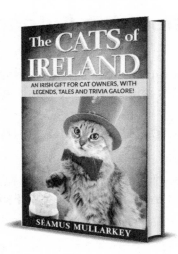

**SCAN TO VIEW
DETAILS...**

More from Seamus Mullarkey

Would you like to read more of my books???
Just click or scan below...

**SCAN TO VIEW
DETAILS...**

More from Seamus Mullarkey

Would you like to read more of my books???
Just click or scan below...

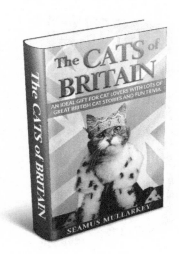

**SCAN TO VIEW
DETAILS...**

... and there's lots more to come ...

Scan the code or click the link so you get notified
the minute I release a new book...

SCAN TO FOLLOW ME

PHOTO CREDITS

1. It Prefers Perrier
White and Black Cat on White Ceramic Bowl
Free to use via Unsplash License -downloaded from
https://unsplash.com/photos/s4ImDgVEi70.

2a. Instead of laying
Croissant Danish Pastry
Free to use via Pixabay License -downloaded from
https://pixabay.com/photos/croissant-danish-pastry-
pastries-1128/

2b. Cat Lying on Green Grass
Creative Commons -downloaded from
https://www.pexels.com/photo/cat-lying-on-green-
grass-385960/.

3. When You promise it
Eiffel Tower Illustration
Creative Commons -downloaded from
https://www.pexels.com/photo/eiffel-tower-
illustration-60027/.

4. It thinks its portrait
Two Brown Cats Wall Decor
Free to use via Unsplash License -downloaded from
https://unsplash.com/photos/B4GzdjVupY0.

5. If It weren't
Tasty Baguette on White Marble Surface
Creative Commons -downloaded from
https://www.pexels.com/photo/tasty-baguette-on-white-marble-surface-5588987/.

6. Like Marie Antoinette
HD Photo by Ashel Mshk
Free to use via Unsplash License -downloaded from
https://unsplash.com/photos/vlliK29z6xo.

7. It knows you eat with the eyes
Ritz London Starter Food
Free to use via Pixabay License -downloaded from
https://pixabay.com/photos/ritz-london-starter-food-ritz-4988164/.

8. And it insists on formal table settings
White and Black Cat on Table
Creative Commons -downloaded from
https://www.pexels.com/photo/white-and-black-cat-on-table-6869554/.

9. It plays with this football
Activities Soccer Sports Purchased
Creative Commons -downloaded from
https://flickr.com/photos/129941959@N06/16099904950/in/photolist-qwGdQ7-Hmzbvh-gFeCW-jhjZ9-4ayrqN-6XtUQ9-c6wp3-cBaQT-3BmGTP-fxoqAD-c6wkG-dLwdN2-73kdv-551QGF-dMw14Z-6q6q4W-6rGZGk-c6TyZ9-4auoPK-c6weH-34ZQQ-556337-bs5ety-73kdz-aKXUke-f6NcsH-5RNY6-dCtB3w-3VsVy-67LWXv-9BPwA9-555Y4E-67LX6B-cRmEvA-551Mxa-67R9rL-67LXMg-dLBEau-67RaQw-qHZ6wk-

cBaMz-pQWQr-dLw7EP-aBVHGs-pQWAw-37HoPE-duUzAV-dLBKcm-6VtNX-2uEM1c.

10. and not this one
Kiagoa Football on Green Grass
Creative Commons -downloaded from
https://www.pexels.com/photo/kigoa-football-on-green-grass-during-daytime-209956/.

11. It thinks of five weeks
Orange Tabby Cat on Gray Blanket
Creative Commons -downloaded from
https://www.pexels.com/photo/orange-tabby-cat-on-gray-blanket-3616232/.

12. Whenever it breaks something
Gray Cat Peeking at the Table
Free to use via Unsplash License -downloaded from
https://unsplash.com/photos/bsSIk3LV_NE.

13. It frequents little neighborhood
Cat in Antofagasta, Chile
Free to use via Unsplash License -downloaded from
https://unsplash.com/photos/wn2BLotE8oY

14. It lives for l 'amour
Brown and Gray Tabby Cats Lying Near the Wall
Creative Commons -downloaded from
https://www.pexels.com/photo/brown-and-gray-tabby-cats-lying-near-the-glass-wall-7726304/.

15. It loves a promenade en bicyclette
Cat Bicycle Animal Outdoors
Free to use via Pixabay License -downloaded from
https://pixabay.com/photos/cat-bicycle-animal-
outdoors-7258257/.

16. Tour de France
Creative Commons -downloaded from
https://flickr.com/photos/sophieffc/2730828163/in/
photolist-5ajd5c-2jJUN6m-2jbnee8-2hLUKfD-RMtapr-
2a41U21-8TCnRR-YKBC9D-dkaJMy-JXXX94-nV82xC-NY2uE5-
YZSsDr-26nPg12-RNDPYf-2mfF4ZW-2ikzBfs-29mqvj-2jJYxj7-
UDkMAz-d9NVwY-2jVZYq7-PAb4Vf-9S6Wdb-2ikNHCf-
2jUbuY2-CQzmXn-2hFMN8m-2jV9BUj-9SiwHc-2iBrdL9-
7X89Tg-nf8L5h-2mMWF7e-2mM6zd2-pfpbaA-oeN5TA-
2jJYuUh-ogwgYa-nXtph9-2jJUTAV-nXfPAL-ay2Kbi-9SmkSb-
9j8n2Y-26XGnpp-oeswFK-nXtv6U-S3YieJ-wCbc7L.

17. It wants to buy books
Cat sleeping among books
Free to use via Unsplash License – downloaded from
https://unsplash.com/photos/bfI9ELZ3vSs

18. It eats rich food
Stretching in the morning
Free to use via Unsplash License – downloaded from
https://unsplash.com/photos/ZlFKIG6dApg

19. It knows how to lounge
short fur orange and black cat
Free to use via Unsplash License – downloaded from
https://unsplash.com/photos/9KpQrPEy8P8

20. It watches French shows on Netflix
Sindy Vonundzu Blitzdings

21. Fresh treats
Cat Macarons

22. It wishes you had a bidet
Red cat

23. It likes long lunches
Close-Up Photography of Short Fur White Kitten

24. It thinks nothing of spending hours
Ginger Cat Sitting on an Outdoor Sofa

25. It shouts "Vive la Revolution"
Silver Tabby Kitten on Floor

26. It read the original French version
three asssorted-color kittens

27. It can analyze the notes in your new perfume
A Cute Cat While Eyes Closed

28. It tends to be rather bureaucratic
Cat Feline Kitty Whiskers

29. It does everything with a certain finesse
A Cat with a Bow Tie

30. Its extensive beauty regime
Brown Tabby Kitten on White Textile

31. It spends hours on park benches
Orange Tabby Cat Lying on Bench

32. It loves to wander along cobblestone
Denise Jans

33. It knows how to accessorize
Russian Blue Cat Wearing Yellow Sunglasses

34. You don't mind if it wakes you early
White Kitten Photo

35. It has a certain je ne sais quoi
One of my cats, Vladimir

36. It makes anything it wears
Cat in Hat Sitting Near Wall

37. It knows how to tie a scarf
Cat Scarf Tabby Warm Portrait

43. It spends August
Young Woman with a Cat on the Beach
Creative Commons -downloaded from
https://www.freepik.com/free-photo/young-woman-with-cat-beach-near-sea-travel-concept-with-pet_24172730.htm#query=cat%20beach&position=2&from_view=search.

44. It perks up if
Dubonnet Alcohol Advert Poster
Creative Commons -downloaded from
https://www.publicdomainpictures.net/en/view-image.php?image=76518&picture=dubonet-alcohol-advert-poster.

45. Cat Wine Vintage Drunk Party
Free to use via Pixabay License -downloaded from
https://pixabay.com/illustrations/cat-wine-vintage-drunk-party-5916926/.

46. It sways in time
White and black cat on green grass
Free to use via Unsplash License – downloaded from
https://unsplash.com/photos/MBgN-CmZEk0

47. It dreams of playing
 Edited Photo of Person Playing Accordion
Free to use via Unsplash License -downloaded from
https://unsplash.com/photos/y2QHMcnCT7Q.

48.It's comfortable hob-nobbing
Black and White of a Man Holding a Cat
Creative Commons -downloaded from
https://www.pexels.com/photo/black-and-white-of-a-man-holding-a-cat-8508905/.

49. It spends hours in the bathroom
Sink of Tula

50. Citroen Ami 6 (1960s)

51. It's all about

52. It's such an intellectual
Cat Monacle Glasses

53. It can't believe
Marco Biondi

54. It thinks of fresh flowers as a necessity

55. It sometimes gets so terribly
Bored Russian Blue by Laura Limsenkhe

56. It likes the loud
Grayscale Photo of a Young Tiger

57. It dreams one day of creating
Orange Cat with Perfume by Tron Le

58.It looks as if
Funny Cat with Mustache

59. It critiques all
close-up photo of brown tabby kitten

60. And then suggests
Clothes Wardrobe Choose

61. It know if it's
Cats and Champagne

62. It prances around the house
Cat Mackerel Watch

63. It yearns for
Cat Animal Window

64. It knows it's all about
Silver Tabby Cat on White Floor Tiles
Free to use via Unsplash License -downloaded from
https://unsplash.com/photos/PAIyI10w_2k

65.It can identify
Cat Cheese
Free to use via Pixabay License -downloaded from
https://pixabay.com/photos/cat-cheese-food-feeding-nature-7300049/.

66. It inspects everything
Orange Fruit on Clear Glass Bowl
Free to use via Unsplash License -downloaded from
https://unsplash.com/photos/UqcTsiZthaQ.

67a. It thinks all
Funny Mime in Black Hat with Thumbs Up
Creative Commons -downloaded from
https://www.freepik.com/free-photo/funny-mime-black-hat-holds-his-thumbs-up_1168468.htm#query=mime&position=6&from_view=search.

67b. It thinks all
Kitten Sweet Cat
Free to use via Pixabay License -downloaded from
https://pixabay.com/photos/kitten-sweet-cat-dancing-jumping-4688244/.

68. It prefers an herbal
Cute Tabby Cat Near an Opened Book and Ceramic Teapot
Creative Commons -downloaded from

https://www.pexels.com/photo/cute-tabby-cat-near-an-opened-book-and-a-ceramic-tea-pot-13413724/.

69a. When it's time to salute
White and Red Flag on Pole La Rochelle, France
Free to use via Unsplash License -downloaded from
https://unsplash.com/photos/LA3nySSuTdA.

69b. When it's time to salute
Cute Animal Mammal
Free to use via Pixabay License -downloaded from
https://pixabay.com/photos/cute-animal-mammal-cat-nature-eye-3210439/.

70. It's tres sportif
Cat Flying to Play
Free to use via Pixabay License -downloaded from
https://pixabay.com/photos/cat-flying-cat-to-play-leap-1680873/.

71. It often seems like
brown tabby cat on teal metal gate
Free to use via Unsplash License – downloaded from
https://unsplash.com/photos/HN3-ehlNwsc

72. It wants you to read it
White and Black Cat on White Book Page
Free to use via Unsplash License -downloaded from
https://unsplash.com/photos/DRNS6gfUI8M.

73. If it doesn't get
Brown and White Cat in Short Focus Shot
Free to use via Unsplash License - downloaded from
https://unsplash.com/photos/tEMU4lzAL0w.

78. It adores
Dancer Painting Ballerina Ballet
Free to use via Pixabay License -downloaded from
https://pixabay.com/photos/dancer-painting-
ballerina-7317099/.

79. It doesn't think much
Cat in Tiara by Robyn Anderson
Creative Commons -downloaded from
https://flickr.com/photos/robynanderson/37228464156/.

80. It reasures la tendresse
Woman in Black and White Leopard Scarf with Brown Long
Fur Cat
Free to use via Unsplash License -downloaded from
https://unsplash.com/photos/AtXEIp_ZIRU

81. It thinks you're rude
Orange and White Tabby Cat Sitting on Brown Wooden Table
in Kitchen
Free to use via Unsplash License -downloaded from
https://unsplash.com/photos/w2DsS-ZAP4U.

82. It hates when you
Selective Focus Photography of Gray Tabby Cat
Free to use via Unsplash License -downloaded from
https://unsplash.com/photos/P_O9wwnMYhg.

83. It greets its friends
Siam Siamese Cat Domestic
Free to use via Pixabay License -downloaded from
https://pixabay.com/photos/siam-siamese-cat-domestic-
cat-puss-2555498/.

84. It's so avant-garde
A Tabby Cat Playing with a String
Creative Commons -downloaded from
https://www.pexels.com/photo/a-tabby-cat-playing-with-a-string-13009744/?fbclid=IwAR3jwJiSrvDM508wE-b58IlVjupuaQFcK9vC-n3KtyraMwZ8t-7Q6sveLDQ.

85. It shows its friends
Cat and Fox Friends by Aleksandr Gorin
Free to use via Unsplash License -downloaded from
https://unsplash.com/photos/c09mHGksRcY.

86. It can't believe the size
Brown Tabby Cat on White Wooden Window
Free to use via Unsplash License -downloaded from
https://unsplash.com/photos/CEx86maLUSc.

87. In its photographs
Cat Domestic Animal cat eyes
Free to use via Pixabay License -downloaded from
https://pixabay.com/photos/cat-domestic-cat-animal-cat-eyes-4157084/.

88. It's considering
Cat Animal Pets Guitar Case
Free to use via Pixabay License -downloaded from
https://pixabay.com/photos/cat-animal-pets-guitar-case-491013/?fbclid=IwAR10R5ikgw0gE3vVD1Z1h0Ug8As3RqxwAg0znEpH13yvtPNwOVCREkPzoec.

89. You suspect it
Top Hat Cat Dance Poster
Creative Commons -downloaded from
https://www.publicdomainpictures.net/en/view-image.php?image=448585&picture=top-hat-cat-dance-poster.

90. It prefers the stairs
brown tabby cat on white stairs
Free to use via Unsplash License – downloaded from
https://unsplash.com/photos/mJaD10XeD7w

91. It despises flip-flops
Diego. Because One Picture Is Never Enough
Creative Commons -downloaded from
https://flickr.com/photos/gomezjaimes/5172025371/in/
photolist-m6ihb-8T2YXe-54QBRi-oa53yh-6MU4bN-2NbdBw-
9MBfNu-Nm1BE-37VjQ-8T6grs-aYQUoc-bz7tw-4XxRx9.

92. It gives you this look
Brown Tabby Cat in Grayscale
Free to use via Unsplash License -downloaded from
https://unsplash.com/photos/3cZFLUUAMnU

93a. It wants to travel to Paris
Bridge and River
Free to use via Unsplash License -downloaded from
https://unsplash.com/photos/wP7XToELmN0.

93b. It wants to travel to Paris
White Siamese Cat
Free to use via Unsplash License -downloaded from
https://unsplash.com/photos/mmAGlgDAXuE.

94. It insists on regular spa days.
Man in Blue Dress Shirt Holding Brown Tabby
Creative Commons -downloaded from
https://www.pexels.com/photo/man-in-blue-dress-shirt-
holding-brown-tabby-cat-6131543/.

95. It prefers lavender
Cat Window Housewall
Free to use via Pixabay License -downloaded from
https://pixabay.com/photos/cat-window-housewall-
lavender-1169300/.

96a. Its fur is as smooth
Chocolate Cupcake on White Ceramic Plate
Free to use via Unsplash License -downloaded from
https://unsplash.com/photos/ChOr35YfmM0.

96b. Its fur is as smooth
Brown Cat Lying on White Textile
Free to use via Unsplash License -downloaded from
https://unsplash.com/photos/15hRe7X1wac.

97a. Although it looks like
Cat staring at me while I was
Free to use via Unsplash License – downloaded from
https://unsplash.com/photos/EWsd0dlKsy0

97b. Although it looks like
Chambord, France by Pierre Antona
Free to use via Unsplash License -downloaded from
https://unsplash.com/photos/El2yIyPqBT8.

98. When you say
If a Wearing Beret and Cape
Creative Commons -downloaded from
https://flickr.com/photos/salihan/2430728814/in/
photolist-29fi-xrRa5B-7Mn6Ma-6X8c3z-4GN7Zu-bD8Vsr-
bD8UJx-bD8USP-bqdZP5-bqe5yf-92QLMV-bD8UcH-bD8Usx-
bD8VcD-93nYvS-bqdZjb-bqe15Q-bD8Voz-bqdZcs-bD8VjK-

bqe5vf-5MXmab-bqdZZd-bD8Uy8-bqdZnu-vebST-qASXZR-
GZe19-5NJcU3-p1vzcV-gcvXu9-4BdA8o-6zMo6q-5L2fmn-
5NLuFL-5L6upY-4GHVzp-q5wpe-5NLuYu-57ksTx-ovic14-bqd-
ZGj-4GN3Gw-6zHmVi-2jdnZAL-4B51AE-6zHmH6-6zHmr4-
ovnnkN-4avrkn.

99. It wants to know precisely
The Boss of the House
Free to use via Unsplash License – downloaded from
https://unsplash.com/photos/RjZjYwimO6Y

100. It hunts but for escargots
Young ginger tom cat in the garden
Free to use via Unsplash License – downloaded from
https://unsplash.com/photos/RjZjYwimO6Y

101. It dreams of la vie en rose
A Cat Surrounded by Flowers
Creative Commons -downloaded from
https://www.pexels.com/photo/a-cat-surrounded-by-
flowers-8551624/.

102. And it never says goodbye
White Cat Lies on Woman's Knees
Creative Commons -downloaded from
https://www.freepik.com/free-photo/white-cat-
lies-woman-s-knees_1472626.htm#query=cat&from_
query=cat%20waving&position=48&from_view=search.

A bientot
Kawaii Icecream Characters

Made in the USA
Coppell, TX
24 February 2024

29362943R00083